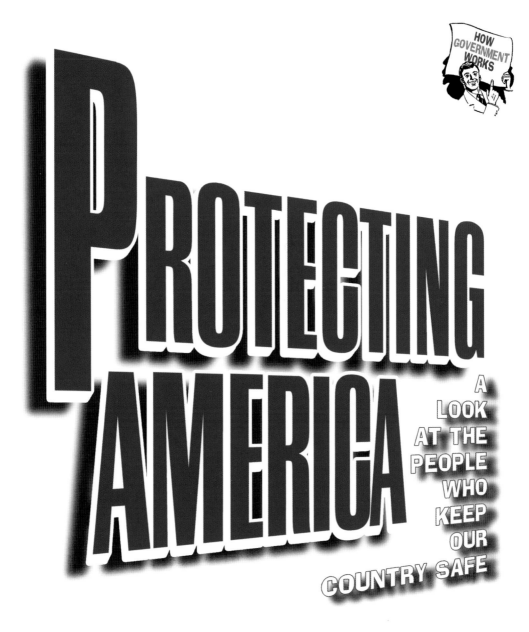

PROTECTING AMERICA

A LOOK AT THE PEOPLE WHO KEEP OUR COUNTRY SAFE

By Sandy Donovan

LERNER PUBLICATIONS COMPANY • MINNEAPOLIS

Lerner Publications Company
A division of Lerner Publishing Group
241 First Avenue North
Minneapolis, MN 55401 U.S.A.

Website address: www.lernerbooks.com

Library of Congress Cataloging-in-Publication Data

Donovan, Sandra, 1967–
        Protecting America : a look at the people who keep our country safe /
by Sandy Donovan.
            p.   cm.—(How government works)
        Includes bibliographical references and index.
        Contents: War and peace: the U.S. Armed Forces—The War on Terrorism:
fighting a threat to world peace—Crossing guards: protecting the nation's
borders—Help! when natural disasters strike—An apple a day: protecting the
public's health—Away from home: keeping Americans safe abroad.
        ISBN: 0-8225-1345-5 (lib. bdg. : alk. paper)
        1. Administrative agencies—United States—Juvenile literature.
2. Terrorism—Prevention—Juvenile literature. 3. Internal security—United
States—Juvenile literature. 4. United States—Armed Forces—Juvenile
literature [1. Administrative Agencies. 2. Terrorism. 3. Internal Security.
4. United States—Armed Forces.] I. Title. II. Series.
        JK421.D66 2004
        363.1'00973—dc21   2002155399

Manufactured in the United States of America
1 2 3 4 5 6 – DP – 09 08 07 06 05 04

TABLE OF CONTENTS

BEING PREPARED IS THE
FIRST STEP OF PROTECTION   4

1. WAR AND PEACE:
   THE U.S. ARMED FORCES   6

2. CROSSING GUARDS: PROTECTING
   THE NATION'S BORDERS   11

3. THE WAR ON TERRORISM: FIGHTING
   A THREAT TO WORLD PEACE   17

4. HELP! WHEN NATURAL
   DISASTERS STRIKE   26

5. AN APPLE A DAY: PROTECTING THE
   PUBLIC'S HEALTH   35

6. AWAY FROM HOME: KEEPING
   AMERICANS SAFE ABROAD   44

   U.S. AGENCIES AND GROUPS THAT
     PROTECT AMERICA   50

   GLOSSARY   51

   SELECTED BIBLIOGRAPHY   52

   FURTHER READING AND WEBSITES   52

   INDEX   54

Introduction: Being Prepared Is the First Step of Protection

THINK ABOUT IT: What is the government's biggest job?

The U.S. government has lots of important jobs. It makes laws, collects taxes, builds schools, and lots more. But in a way, laws, taxes, and all the other things that the government does have the same goal: to help protect citizens. Protecting citizens is one of the biggest duties of the government.

(Above) A Michigan state police officer *(left)* and an agent from the bureau that specializes in guns and bombs *(right)* discuss a crisis.

You can probably think of all kinds of things that people need to be protected from: wars, violence, disasters, and diseases. The government works hard to protect citizens from all of these threats. The government is made up of experts in many different areas. These experts know the best way to protect citizens from any particular threat.

One of the most important ways that the government protects people is by making sure that some of these threats never reach us. For instance, the army doesn't just fight wars. It also tries to prevent, or stop, wars before they start. Other parts of the government work to stop criminals and enemies before they commit acts such as the September 11, 2001, attacks on New York City and Washington, D.C. People in the government work around the clock to find ways to predict natural disasters such as earthquakes. They also study ways to prevent diseases from spreading around the country.

The government tries hard to keep threats from reaching U.S. citizens. Knowing how the government works to protect people can make us all feel safer.

CHAPTER 1
WAR AND PEACE:
THE U.S. ARMED FORCES

TRUE OR FALSE? During times of peace, members of the U.S. armed forces spend a lot of time watching television.

FALSE! The armed forces have just as much to do in peaceful times as they do during wars.

When people think about protecting our country, many of them imagine wars. A war is a fight between one country and another. Most countries have armed forces with trained soldiers, sailors, and pilots to fight wars. So people might picture tanks rolling

U.S. soldiers march in formation.

over battlefields, fighter jets zooming through the sky, or submarines emerging from the sea to look for enemy boats.

But fighting wars is just one part of what the armed forces do to protect us. The armed forces, also called the military, include the U.S. Army, the U.S. Navy, the U.S. Air Force, and the U.S. Marine Corps. These four branches of the armed forces do fight wars. They always have to be ready to defend the country. But they also help to keep the peace. (A fifth service, the U.S. Coast Guard, also takes part in

A U.S. Air Force F-16 fighter plane

defense. However, it usually does not play a big role in wars. Its job focuses most on keeping U.S. waters safe.)

Sometimes the United States fights wars in order to keep peace in the long run. In March 2003, U.S. troops went to war in Iraq, a nation in southwestern Asia. U.S. leaders said that Iraq's government, led by President Saddam Hussein, was hiding dangerous chemical and nuclear weapons. By fighting a war against Iraq, the U.S. government hoped to prevent Hussein from using those weapons against other countries or against his own people. That way, the future would be safer and more peaceful.

In Times of War

The United States is a huge country, and the armed forces have a huge job. Fighting wars is the first part of the armed services' mission, or purpose. In wartime the army, navy, air force, and marines concentrate on defending the United

States. To do this job, they have thousands of top-notch men and women who are trained and ready for action. If the United States is attacked, members of the armed services can be sent to any part of the world on short notice. The armed forces also have some of the most complicated equipment available. Scientists and other inventors work constantly to keep this equipment up to date.

TURNING POINT Both men and women can join the U.S. armed forces. But for a long time, women were not allowed to fight in battle. Since the 1990s, however, women have slowly started to play a bigger role in battle. They fly fighter jets and helicopters, lead troops, and serve on battleships.

Getting the thousands of armed forces' members ready for work is a big job in itself. The U.S. Department of Defense, a department in the national government, is in charge of the armed forces. It takes care of training all U.S. service members and giving them uniforms,

The fast attack submarine USS *Salt Lake City (bottom)* pulls close to a ship *(top)* that is specially equipped to service submarines at sea. Some U.S. Navy submarines can travel for years without refueling. Their tools are among the best in the world. They use high-powered tracking devices to find objects hundreds of miles away.

DRAFTED FOR SERVICE

All new members of the U.S. armed services are volunteers. They have decided for themselves that they want to sign up for the military. But joining the armed services has not always been voluntary. During some wars, the military has needed more soldiers than have volunteered. The government passed laws that allowed the armed forces to pick people for service. This system was called the draft. Men have been drafted during many wars, including the Civil War (1861–1865), the two World Wars (1914–1918 and 1939–1945), and the Vietnam War (1961–1975). Women have never been drafted, and there has not been a draft since 1973. But all American men still register for the draft. If the government needs more people to join the military in the future, it can begin drafting again.

weapons, and other equipment. New members are called recruits. They go through hard training before they are ready to serve in any branch of the armed forces. The training makes sure that service members are physically fit and mentally prepared to do their job.

You may have an idea of how the different branches of the armed forces fight wars. For the most part, the army is on the ground, the navy and the marines are at sea, and the air force is in the sky. But it's not quite that simple. For example many members of the navy actually fly fighter jets. And some army soldiers are specially trained to parachute from planes into battle areas.

IN TIMES OF PEACE

Most of the time, the United States is not involved in any wars. What do the armed services do then?

SPECIAL OPS

In addition to the four main branches of the armed forces, the U.S. military also has units called special operations forces (special ops). The U.S. Navy SEALS are one type of special operations force. SEALS are among the most highly skilled soldiers in the world. They go through intense training at sea, on land, and in the air. In fact, their name stands for SEa, Air, and Land. Like other members of the U.S. military, SEALS are sent on missions in both peacetime and wartime. They use special skills such as parachuting and scuba diving to get into territory that other soldiers can't reach.

During peacetime, members of the armed forces perform an even more valuable service than fighting: they keep the peace. U.S. military bases are located all over the world. Many of them are in places where the United States has never fought a war. Sometimes U.S. Navy ships patrol waters where there is no fighting. And thousands of U.S. soldiers live on army bases in countries with whom the United States is friendly. Other countries are less likely to start a war if they see that the U.S. armed forces are strong around the world.

Another part of the U.S. armed forces' mission is to help out when a disaster strikes. When a hurricane or some other natural disaster hits the United States, members of the armed services are often among the first on the scene. They direct citizens to safety and make sure that buildings are safe.

Did You KNOW? The U.S. armed forces help out when disasters strike other nations, too. U.S. forces are often among the first to respond.

CHAPTER 2
CROSSING GUARDS: PROTECTING THE NATION'S BORDERS

QUICK QUESTION: Have you ever traveled to another country?

If you live close to Mexico or Canada, you may go there often. Or maybe you've never crossed from one country to another.

(Above) People cross between Canada and the United States at Niagara Falls every day— but not usually on a tightrope.

The edges of a country are called its borders. Borders can be land, water, or even air. The United States has long land borders with Canada and Mexico and long water borders along the Atlantic and Pacific Oceans.

DIG DEEPER The southern tip of Florida has the most heavily guarded water borders in the United States. This is because many people try to escape poverty in the tiny island country of Cuba by swimming or boating to Florida.

When you think about protecting a country's borders, you may picture the armed forces keeping off invading enemies. But invasions have rarely been a threat to the United States. The United States is friendly with its closest neighbors, and other invaders would have to come from far away. Even though part of the military's job is to protect U.S. borders, the armed forces do not have to spend very much time doing this work. Most of the time, other countries do not try to attack the United States because they know how strong the U.S. armed forces are.

If other countries are unlikely to attack, why do U.S. borders need protection? Other threats can also enter the United States by crossing its borders. Terrorists—people who commit acts of violence to force a government to do something—are one of these threats. The United States wants to keep any suspected terrorists out of the country.

Other dangers may threaten U.S. borders, too. Some people try to hide illegal items and bring them into the United States. These people are called smugglers. Many of the things that they smuggle, such as drugs, can be harmful. The U.S. government wants to protect its citizens by keeping these items out of the country.

BORDER PATROL: POLICING U.S. BORDERS

The Border Patrol's job is to make sure that smugglers do not bring illegal items into the United States. Most Border Patrol workers wear uniforms and work at checkpoints along the U.S. borders with Mexico and Canada. Agents at highway checkpoints search cars, trucks, and buses before these vehicles enter the United States. The agents look for smuggled drugs. They also watch for illegal immigrants—people who are trying to sneak into the United States from other countries.

A Border Patrol officer searches a man for illegal drugs.

DANGEROUS JOURNEYS

Sometimes smugglers try to sneak people into the United States. U.S. laws say that people can only immigrate (move to the United States from other countries) with the government's permission. Only a certain number of immigrants are allowed in each year. But many more people want to immigrate than are allowed. People who live in poor countries want to move to the United States to find work. Many of them pay smugglers to help them get past the Border Patrol.

But some smugglers don't care about the safety of the immigrants. They may crowd them into vehicles without enough air or lead them through unclean tunnels. In fact, many people have died trying to make the trip from Mexico to the United States. In addition to wanting to prevent illegal immigrants from entering the United States, Border Patrol officers also want to protect the immigrants from smugglers who might hurt them or put them in danger.

This X ray of a truck at the border between Mexico and the United States reveals people huddled inside. They are probably illegal immigrants.

Other Border Patrol agents work undercover. They don't wear uniforms, and they don't let strangers know that they are agents. They try to catch smugglers by surprise. They patrol the areas around the U.S. borders in cars, planes, and boats, as well as on foot and on horseback.

The Border Patrol has plenty of work patrolling the U.S. land borders with Canada and Mexico. But many of the borders are water, not land. The main job of patrolling these water borders belongs to the Coast Guard.

DIG DEEPER Being a Border Patrol agent takes hard work. All agents have to pass a written test and go to training school for five months. They also have to learn Spanish in order to work along the Mexican border.

COAST GUARD: THE POLICE AND AMBULANCE OF U.S. WATERS

The U.S. Coast Guard is not part of the Border Patrol. It is actually the smallest branch of the armed services. Like the other branches of the service, its main job is to protect the United States. And, like the other branches, the Coast Guard is not only active in wartime. The Coast Guard is always on the lookout for illegal activities in U.S. waters. U.S. laws give the Coast Guard the right to search any suspicious ships or boats for illegal items. Coast Guard officials are often called the police of the seas.

Coast Guard members are also always on the lookout for anyone in U.S. waters who needs help. If a boat accident takes place, the Coast Guard is often the first to arrive and give help. For this reason, the Coast Guard is

**Did You?
KNOW:** On an average day, members of the U.S. Coast Guard save 10 lives and help more than 190 people.

also called the ambulance of the seas.

Coast Guard members have to be trained for all kinds of emergencies. If a huge oil tanker catches fire off the coast of Alaska, Coast Guard boats rush to the scene. Some Coast Guard members might be firefighters, who put out the fire. Others may be rescue workers, who help rescue the tanker's crewmembers. Other Coast Guard members may use search equipment to locate missing crewmembers, who may be in lifeboats or swimming in the water around the ship. They do whatever they can to help people reach safety.

A Coast Guard team attempts to board the fishing trawler (boat) *Alaska Patriot*. It had engine trouble.

CHAPTER 3
THE WAR ON TERRORISM: FIGHTING A THREAT TO WORLD PEACE

THINK ABOUT IT: More than three thousand people died as a result of terrorist attacks in New York City and Washington, D.C., on September 11, 2001. It was the largest terrorist strike ever on U.S. soil. Do you remember what you were doing when you heard about the attacks?

On that morning, terrorists hijacked four airplanes and crashed three of them into buildings. In New York, the famous World Trade Center was in ruins. In Washington, D.C., the mighty Pentagon—the home base of the U.S. armed forces—had a giant

The September 11, 2001, terrorist attack set fire to the twin towers of the World Trade Center (right).

hole on one side. You've probably seen pictures from that day. Thousands of people ran through the streets of New York, trying to escape the falling towers of the Trade Center. People say that it was a day that changed the world forever.

This attack against America was not the kind of attack that most people had ever thought about very much. It had taken the country completely by surprise. President George W. Bush said afterward that the country was facing a new kind of war. This was a war on terrorism. Terrorism often targets civilians (people who are not in the armed forces or other government jobs). How would the country fight this new kind of war?

"**SOUND BYTE**" "Terrorist attacks can shake the foundations of our biggest buildings, but they cannot touch the foundation of America. These acts shatter steel, but they cannot dent the steel of American resolve."
—President George W. Bush on September 11, 2001

RUSHING TO THE RESCUE

One of the first things the government wanted to do on September 11 was to save as many people as possible. Thousands of people had been in the World Trade Center when the two planes struck its towers. The towers contained hundreds of offices, shops, and restaurants. Many people also worked in the Pentagon. Soon people from all over the country joined the rescue missions in New York and Washington, D.C. Civilians who wanted

A firefighter views the mess on a street in New York City after the terrorist attack on the World Trade Center.

to help joined firefighters, police officers, and members of the armed services.

Once the rescue mission was under way, the government had another job. It had to make sure that an attack like this one would not happen again.

At a Michigan airport, a police officer guides a specially trained dog who sniffs luggage for explosives (bombs).

Just as keeping the peace is sometimes more important than fighting wars, preventing terrorism can be more important than fighting terrorists. The government wants to stop terrorists before they attack the United States. To do this, the president works with a group called the National Security Council. This group is made up of leaders from other areas in the government. They work together to develop ways to keep the country safe.

THE FBI: FIGHTING CRIMINALS

The National Security Council gets help from many government agencies (specialized offices) to try to prevent harmful acts such as terrorism. The Federal Bureau of Investigation (FBI) is one of these agencies. The FBI is the law enforcement branch of the federal (national) government. When the FBI was created in 1908, it investigated national crimes such as bank robbery and kidnapping.

Over the years, the types of crimes that people committed began to change. People started to commit very complicated crimes. Some of them used modern technology.

J. Edgar Hoover *(center)* was the director of the FBI from 1924 to 1972. In this 1938 photo, he reviews documents about a kidnapping with his staff.

Large groups of criminals also formed to commit detailed crimes, such as earning money illegally and hiding it from the government. This type of crime is called organized crime, and it often involves earning money from gambling and illegal drugs.

As crimes have changed, so has the FBI. The FBI handles more than 350 kinds of crimes. These crimes are divided into a few main groups, including organized crime, violent crime, foreign counterintelligence (spying and other efforts by foreign countries to find out secret U.S. information), and terrorism.

Since the September 11 terrorist acts, the FBI has become more involved in fighting terrorism. FBI agents help to identify people around the world whom they suspect of being terrorists. They watch what these people do and with whom they meet. Agents try to find out if any of these people are planning terrorist attacks. Then they share this information with other parts of the U.S. government, such as the Customs Service.

The Customs Service's job is to make sure that every person who comes into the United States is allowed to do so. With help from the FBI, customs agents can try to prevent suspected terrorists from entering the country. Doing this is one of the best ways to prevent future acts of terrorism in the United States.

TOOLS OF THE TRADE

U.S. crime-fighting agencies have many tools to help them do their jobs. For example, the FBI collects millions of fingerprint records. Fingerprints are the pattern of lines on the pads of your fingertips. Everyone's fingerprints are unique. No two people in the world have the same fingerprints! FBI agents compare fingerprint records to fingerprints at crime scenes to identify and catch terrorists and criminals.

DNA is another amazing crime-fighting tool. DNA is a chemical code that describes everything physical about a person—hair color, eye color, height, and more. Like fingerprints, DNA is unique. If two DNA samples are the same, that means they came from the same person. Sometimes this code helps the FBI and other agencies crack tough cases.

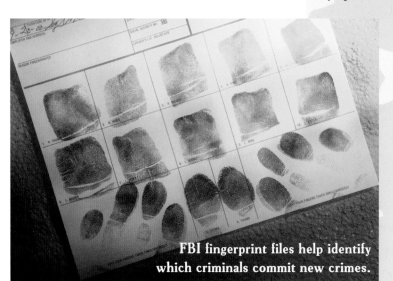

FBI fingerprint files help identify which criminals commit new crimes.

Many CIA agents spend their time watching other people.

THE CIA: SPYING AND MORE

The U.S. government also wants to prevent terrorists from operating in other countries. They get help from the Central Intelligence Agency (CIA). You may have heard of the CIA. Maybe you picture CIA agents wearing trench coats, running around foreign countries, spying on enemies, and sending coded messages back to Washington, D.C. This is often how we see CIA agents in movies. And, in fact, many CIA agents really do work this way. Their job is to find out as much as they can about any outside threats to America's security. They may watch people or listen in on conversations to find out an enemy's secrets. Then agents pass this information on to the president and the National Security Council.

In addition to the FBI and the CIA, the U.S. Department of State—also called the State Department— handles relations between the United States and other countries. The State Department's main job is to try to keep peace between the United States and other nations.

HOMELAND SECURITY

The way the U.S. government works has changed as a result of September 11. Less than one month after the attacks, President Bush created a new office of the national government, called the Office of Homeland Security. The president appointed Pennsylvania's governor, Tom Ridge, to head this office. His mission is to help develop a national plan to prevent more terrorist attacks on Americans.

The president also asked the government to create a whole new department, called the Department of Homeland Security. This brand-new department became official in November 2002, when President Bush signed the Homeland Security Act. The department will try to bring together information from all of the government agencies that already work to protect Americans. In addition to trying to prevent future terrorist attacks, the Department of Homeland Security will work to reduce the damage caused by any future attacks.

Tom Ridge *(second from left)*, the director of Homeland Security, speaks to reporters at a training center for disaster response teams.

Sometimes the department also works to prevent fighting among other countries, to help keep world peace. The State Department has headquarters in Washington, D.C., and offices in more than 250 cities around the world.

The military also plays a role in the fight against terrorism. After September 11, the U.S. armed forces were sent to fight the government of Afghanistan, a country in central Asia. Afghanistan's government had supported many of the terrorists who had been involved in the attacks. The State Department took part in the fight, too. It went to work getting other countries to join America's war on terrorism. This war is a group effort by the military, law enforcement agencies such as the FBI, the State Department, and many other parts of the U.S. government.

PEOPLE FILE The terrorist group al-Qaeda, led by Osama bin Laden, was behind the September 11 attacks. But even before then, bin Laden had been on the FBI's Ten Most Wanted list. He was suspected of plotting terrorist bombings in Africa in 1998 that killed more than two hundred people.

WHEN THE EARTH SHAKES

Earthquakes are natural disasters that cause the earth's surface to shake. Scientists cannot predict earthquakes, and there is no way to prevent them. They happen along fault lines—places where the earth's surface is not stable. Fault lines make some areas more likely to have earthquakes than others. In the United States, a major fault line called the San Andreas Fault runs through California. In January 1994, the Northridge Earthquake struck southern California about twenty miles from Los Angeles. This earthquake killed fifty-seven people, injured nine thousand, and caused billions of dollars' worth of damage. It was the worst earthquake in recent U.S. history.

help keep people from getting hurt during earthquakes. FEMA also teaches people how to keep their homes and cars safe in natural disasters.

An earthquake damaged this highway. Can you see what happened to the double line across the middle?

Local groups also help people get ready for natural disasters. For instance, if you live in an area where hurricanes are common, firefighters might come to your school to teach you what to do if there's ever a hurricane. They may talk about how to try to keep yourself and your home safe. Local police departments also train their members about how to prevent damage from disasters and how to recover from them.

Sometimes, if a natural disaster is expected, the National Guard may be called in to help local groups and FEMA workers. The National Guard is part of the national government. The guard is like a reserve police

A national guardsman looks over a pile of cars thrown together and damaged by a hurricane in Miami, Florida.

A line of National Guard vehicles carries food, water, cots, and medical supplies to a disaster site in North Carolina. National Guard units in every state are always ready to help.

force. Each state recruits its own members, and the federal government pays for them. National Guard members can help people prepare for many disasters. If a large flood is on its way, the guard may help people line a river's banks with huge bags of sand. These bags can help keep floodwaters from spilling over. If it doesn't look like the sandbags will be enough to keep the water away, National Guard members can help people evacuate, or move to safer areas.

Flood control along the Mississippi River in the central United States is a frequent National Guard job. When the Mississippi River flooded the area in 2001, people stacked up more than one million sandbags along the river's banks.

AFTER THE STORM

Although many natural disasters can be predicted, they cannot be prevented. They will happen whether we want them to or not. FEMA workers, firefighters, police officers, and National Guard members can try to make sure that no one is killed or injured in a disaster. But it is almost impossible to keep houses and buildings from being damaged. So, after a flood, a tornado, a hurricane, or an earthquake, people need help recovering and rebuilding.

The same people who teach communities how to prepare for disasters also take part in recovery. After a disaster, local fire and police departments spring into action right away. First, they make sure that anyone who has been injured gets to the hospital for care. Sometimes hospitals have to call in extra doctors and nurses if a lot of people have been injured. Once these people are being helped, firefighters and police then try to figure out how much damage has been done. They may start to clean up the area.

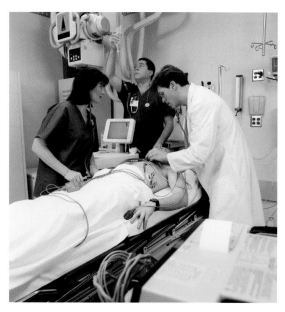

Everyone's first priority after a natural disaster is to make sure injured people get care. Doctors and nurses have to act fast.

If a natural disaster has caused a great deal of destruction, the governor of a state may ask the president for help. If the president thinks the damage is bad enough, the president declares that the area is officially a disaster area. Then FEMA is called in.

FEMA workers help disaster victims find places to stay if their homes have been damaged or destroyed. They also help repair homes and work with local officials to fix city office buildings that have been damaged.

A FEMA worker (right) unloads supplies after a hurricane in Virginia.

The National Guard also helps out after disasters. They can bring emergency supplies into areas where the roads are bad. They may also help clean up if a lot of property has been damaged. They may also help get people to safe places, out of the way of danger. They have special vehicles and highly trained people for just these sorts of duties.

SPACE SHUTTLE *COLUMBIA* DISASTER

In February 2003, the space shuttle *Columbia* broke apart in flight, and pieces of the shuttle fell to the ground in Texas and Louisiana. President George W. Bush declared a state of emergency, and FEMA workers went to help with cleanup. But cleaning up did not just mean picking up the shuttle parts. They had to be saved and studied. Scientists hoped they could keep other shuttles safe by understanding what went wrong on the *Columbia*. So workers had to make sure that no one took pieces or damaged them in any way. Workers also knew that some of the shuttle pieces might hold dangerous chemicals. FEMA workers made sure that the public stayed safe.

Fallen pieces from the space shuttle *Columbia* started brush fires.

Often the American Red Cross helps out after a disaster, too. The Red Cross is not part of the government. However, it works closely with government agencies like FEMA, the National Guard, and the fire and police departments to help people recover after a disaster. The Red Cross may set up shelters where people can stay if their homes have been destroyed. Red Cross workers can also provide basic medical care. Together, the Red Cross, local agencies, the National Guard, and FEMA work to help people before and after natural disasters.

A Red Cross volunteer helps a family after a flood in Pembroke Pines, Florida.

CHAPTER 5
AN APPLE A DAY: PROTECTING THE PUBLIC'S HEALTH

QUICK QUESTION: Did you know that doctors and nurses are also detectives?

Sometimes health-care workers have to put together a lot of clues to figure out what is making a patient ill. Consider the following case.

In the summer of 1999, a man living in New York City went to see his doctor. The man had not been feeling quite right for a few weeks. He'd had a headache, body

(Above) Workers in medical laboratories often help doctors solve medical mysteries.

aches, and a slight fever. He wasn't feeling terrible, but he couldn't seem to get rid of these aches. His doctor examined him but couldn't find anything wrong.

The man went home, but he didn't start feeling any better. A month later, he went to see his doctor again. He told him he still felt the same: headache, body aches, and a little fever. This time, the doctor had just read about a new disease that was popping up around the city: the West Nile virus. Its symptoms were very much like the ones his patient described.

The doctor tested his patient's blood and discovered that he did indeed have the West Nile virus. He was only the fifteenth person in the United States to ever have this disease. The West Nile virus had been infecting people in Africa since the 1930s. But until the summer of 1999, no one had ever had the disease in the United States.

LEARN THE LINGO

The West Nile virus is named after the Nile River, the longest river in Africa.

Doctors knew that the West Nile virus was spread when mosquitoes bit sick birds and then bit humans. They knew that some people who had the virus got very sick. Their spinal cords and their brains could swell. People could even die from the disease. Doctors also knew that people with the virus had to get to the hospital so they could be treated quickly if they did become seriously ill. But they didn't know how to prevent the disease or how to cure it. People got very worried when the disease began showing up in the United States.

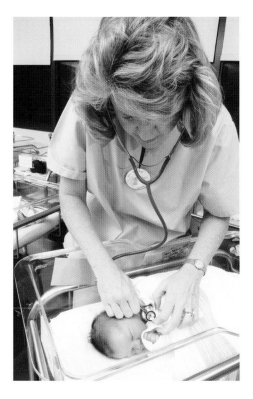

America's youngest citizens need special protection from epidemics.

EPIDEMICS: THE FAST DISEASES

A disease such as the West Nile virus, with no known way to stop it or cure it, can cause a deadly epidemic. An epidemic is an outbreak of a disease that spreads quickly through a community, making more and more people sick. Hundreds of years ago, bubonic plague epidemics killed millions of people in Europe. Epidemics can destroy whole countries if too many people get very sick in a short time. A serious epidemic can be a bigger threat to a country than wars or natural disasters put together.

The United States has not had very many epidemics. The government works hard to control serious diseases before they can spread very far or become epidemics. Government doctors and scientists study diseases and other health problems to find ways to prevent them and to cure them. The main agency that does these jobs is the Centers for Disease Control and Prevention (CDC), a part of the U.S. Department of Health and Human Services.

PEOPLE FILE In July 2002, Dr. Julie L. Gerberding became the CDC's first female director.

PROTECT YOURSELF

When the West Nile virus appeared in the United States, many people were scared. But the CDC did not want them to panic. CDC doctors and workers knew that people would feel safer if they knew a few simple ways to avoid the virus. They also knew that educating the public to protect itself is one of the government's biggest and most important jobs.

Because mosquitoes could spread the virus, the CDC decided to teach people how they could avoid being bitten by the insects. They knew that everyone—even kids—could take a few simple steps to protect themselves. Here are some tips from the CDC on what you can do to stay safe:

> You don't have to stay inside all day to avoid mosquito bites. When you're doing sports, playing in the park, or just taking a walk, dress smart. Wear long sleeves and long pants when you can. Hats help, too. And choose light colors—mosquitoes don't like them as much as dark ones.

> Of course, you can't cover up all your skin all the time. So for extra protection, wear mosquito repellent. Have an adult help you put it on, and make sure that you don't get it in your eyes or mouth. After putting on repellent, always wash your hands.

> Be extra careful around sunrise and sunset—lots of mosquitoes like to come out at those times.

> Watch out for places with standing water, such as flowerpot holders, wading pools, beach buckets, and other containers. Lots of mosquitoes make nests in these wet spots. If you can, dump out extra water that's sitting around in your yard or home.

It's easy to protect yourself. Share these simple ideas with your family and friends, too. You'll be helping the CDC do its job!

The headquarters of the CDC is in Atlanta, Georgia.

The CDC is based in Atlanta, Georgia. Its mission is to protect the health and safety of U.S. citizens. More than 8,500 people work for this agency. They collect information about all kinds of health threats and look for cures. They also look for ways to prevent public health problems. When the West Nile virus broke out, for example, CDC workers helped spread information on how to avoid being bitten by mosquitoes.

CDC workers faced another challenge in 2003. A serious new disease had appeared in China. People were coming down with high fevers, terrible coughs, and bad headaches. Some of them had to go to the hospital for a long time. Some people died.

Doctors did not know what was causing this sickness,

PROTECTING THE EARTH PROTECTS PEOPLE'S HEALTH

The U.S. Environmental Protection Agency (EPA) is another national agency that works to keep Americans healthy. The EPA's mission is to protect the country's natural environment— the air, the land, and the water. For instance, the EPA makes laws about how much pollution companies are allowed to dump into rivers. This helps to keep America's rivers clean. And cleaner rivers are better for the health of the people and animals that use those rivers for drinking water.

which they called Severe Acute Respiratory Syndrome (SARS). At first, they weren't sure how it was spread. But they did know that it was spreading fast—fast enough to be an epidemic.

Soon SARS had spread beyond China. Travelers got sick and carried the disease to other countries. Only a few cases of SARS had shown up in the United States. But the CDC wanted to make sure that Americans knew how to stay healthy. CDC workers also wanted to educate people about what symptoms to watch for. That way, if someone did get sick, he or she could get help right away, before passing the disease to anyone else. The CDC worked hard to help keep people safe from SARS.

In addition to tackling national health threats, the CDC also works with local health departments across the

Many travelers at international airports wear masks to protect themselves from SARS.

country. These include state, county, and city health departments. If there is a health threat in one city, the local health department can get help from the CDC to fight it.

The CDC may help teach people how to deal with the threat. For instance, many diseases are caused by harmful germs that can live in certain kinds of food. When people know how to handle these foods, they can help prevent the diseases.

BIOTERRORISM

The CDC is also involved in the war on terrorism. Doctors and scientists are working to help prevent a certain kind of terrorism called bioterrorism. Bioterrorism does not involve

A hotel manager *(far right)* inspects a hotel restaurant kitchen. He wants to make sure the chef cooks food under healthy conditions.

the kind of violence that we usually think of as terrorism. Instead, bioterrorism is the spread of tiny living things called organisms. These organisms often contain diseases

Weapons against Disease

Have you ever gone to the doctor's office for a checkup and found out that you needed some shots? These shots were probably vaccines. You may not enjoy these quick needle pricks at the doctor's office. But vaccines do a lot to protect you. Vaccines are tiny amounts of certain diseases that have been treated to make them safe. When a disease is injected into your blood as a vaccine, it shouldn't make you sick. But it does give your body a way to fight the disease later on, if you come in contact with it.

Americans are vaccinated against many different diseases. For instance, all American children can be vaccinated against polio. In the early to mid-1900s, polio caused thousands of children to be paralyzed so they could not walk. There was no known cure, and polio was a scary word for children and their parents. But thanks to the polio vaccine developed by Jonas Salk in the 1950s, this disease is no longer a threat.

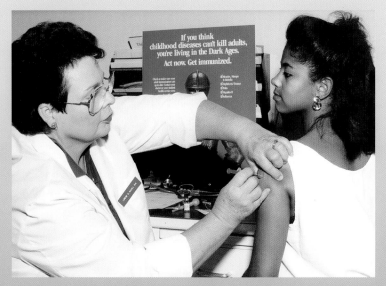

Some vaccines need be repeated after a period of years to keep protecting people's health.

such as smallpox or the West Nile virus. Bioterrorists try to spread these diseases by sending the organisms over a wide area. This action can make thousands or even millions of people sick at once.

Soon after the September 11 attacks, some Americans received mail with anthrax spores in it. These spores were organisms that could give people anthrax, a very serious disease. People across the United States were afraid that they would receive a letter or package carrying these tiny, deadly particles. They believed that the anthrax spores were being sent through the mail on purpose as an act of bioterrorism. The CDC immediately went to work to try to identify and prevent the spread of anthrax.

DIG DEEPER

In January 2003, President George W. Bush proposed Project BioShield. If other members of the government approve the project, it will focus on studying bioterrorism and developing ways to protect Americans against it.

Government doctors and scientists have their hands full protecting public health. It takes a great deal of time and effort to keep people healthy and to fight threats like epidemics and bioterrorism. But the U.S. government has some of the world's best equipment and most highly skilled people to handle the job.

CHAPTER 6
AWAY FROM HOME: KEEPING AMERICANS SAFE ABROAD

QUICK QUESTION: Did you know that the United States has more than 130 embassies in countries around the world?

Embassies act like small branches of the U.S. government in other countries. Embassy workers help to maintain peace around the world and to take care of U.S. citizens who are living or traveling abroad. But sometimes

(Above) **The U.S. embassy in London, England**

embassies themselves are threatened. Think about the following true story.

It was about 10:30 in the morning on August 8, 1998. Two members of the U.S. Marines pulled up in front of the U.S. embassy in Nairobi, Kenya, in Africa. The embassy in Nairobi was a seven-story concrete building. Hundreds of people were working there that morning.

The two marines were off duty that day. They were just stopping by the embassy to cash a check. One of them, Staff Sergeant Daniel Briehl, waited in the car while the other one, Sergeant Jesse Aliganga, walked into the embassy. Sergeant Aliganga walked past another marine sergeant, who was on duty guarding the embassy, and stepped into the elevator to go up to the bank.

Suddenly, an explosion ripped through the building. A terrorist had backed a truck full of explosives into the rear wall of the embassy. Smoke and fire filled the embassy.

Sergeant Jesse Aliganga
died in the attack in 1998.

From outside, Sergeant Briehl heard the blast and saw smoke billowing out of the building's windows. He rushed inside to help, and he found a scary situation. The strength of the blast had knocked out some people. Others were injured or choking from the smoke. Frightened people were trying to escape the burning building.

PROTECTING EMBASSIES

As a marine, Sergeant Briehl was trained to act in emergencies like this one. Marines guard U.S. embassies around the world. Their job is to protect the buildings and the people who work there from attacks of any kind. But, like all threats, some dangers cannot be expected or prevented. They can catch even highly guarded embassies by surprise. Sometimes terrorists attack U.S. embassies as a way of scaring people and of showing their anger against the United States. This is what happened that day in Kenya. A total of 212 people were killed, including Sergeant Aliganga. That same

DOGS ON DUTY

The job of guarding U.S. embassies around the world is divided among many agencies. Even the Department of the Treasury—the agency that prints U.S. money—is involved in keeping embassies safe. That's because the Treasury Department oversees the Bureau of Alcohol, Tobacco, Firearms, and Explosives. The bureau is mostly responsible for keeping track of guns within the United States, but it also has a special program called the Explosives Detection Canine Program. In this program, dogs are trained to sniff out bombs before they are used. Most of these special dogs are used by local law enforcement agencies, but some end up guarding embassies around the world.

A U.S. marine keeps watch at the gate to the U.S. embassy in Kabul, Afghanistan.

day, 11 more people died in a terrorist bombing at the U.S. embassy in Tanzania, also in Africa.

Other times, people hold protests outside embassies when they disagree with U.S. actions. Sometimes these protests turn into fights, and people get injured or killed. The U.S. Marines are often on hand to deal with these kinds of situations.

The United Nations did not support the U.S.-led war against Iraq in 2003. Protesters gathered outside many U.S. embassies to express their anger.

While protecting U.S. embassies is a small part of the Marine Corps' duties—less than one-tenth of all marines have this job—it is a very important task. U.S. embassies create an image of America's strength in other countries. They also provide information about traveling to the United States.

PROTECTING TRAVELERS

Protecting all U.S. citizens in foreign countries—not just those who work in embassies—is also an important task of the U.S. government. U.S. citizens travel to dozens of countries around the world. Many of these places are fascinating to visit. But many of them also have unstable governments or poor health care. Americans traveling to foreign countries could find themselves caught in the middle of an unexpected war. Or they could find themselves suddenly very ill, with no doctor to be found.

Not all emergencies can be avoided. But being informed of the conditions in foreign countries can help American travelers protect themselves from many threats. To keep U.S. citizens up to date, the State Department helps travelers get information about conditions in other countries. The department issues warnings about traveling in certain countries. These warnings tell travelers about potential

DIG DEEPER The State Department posts information on its website for students planning to travel to countries around the world. The web information includes warnings about wars and health threats. The State Department also gives general information about foreign cultures with which Americans may not be familiar.

threats, such as war or political problems. Sometimes warnings advise travelers who are already in a country to leave immediately. Other times, warnings tell people about diseases that they are likely to encounter in certain countries. Sometimes people have to get certain vaccines before they travel. The vaccines help ensure that American travelers won't get sick and also that they won't carry back diseases to the United States.

When travelers do run into trouble in foreign countries, they can always head to the nearest U.S. embassy for help and information. Embassies try to protect U.S. citizens who are traveling and working abroad in the same ways that the U.S. government protects its citizens at home. Protection against health threats, natural disasters, terrorism, and war are all part of that job. It takes cooperation among many highly trained workers to keep Americans safe at home and around the world.

Did You KNOW? Just as the United States has embassies around the world, other countries have embassies in the United States, too. More than 150 foreign embassies are located in Washington, D.C.

U.S. Agencies and Groups that Protect America

Armed forces: Air Force, Army, Coast Guard, Marine Corps, and Navy

Border Patrol

Bureau of Alcohol, Tobacco, Firearms, and Explosives

Centers for Disease Control and Prevention (CDC)

Central Intelligence Agency (CIA)

Customs Service

Department of Defense

Department of Health and Human Services

Department of Homeland Security

Department of State (also known as the State Department)

Department of the Treasury

Environmental Protection Agency (EPA)

Federal Bureau of Investigation (FBI)

Federal Emergency Management Agency (FEMA)

National Guard

National Security Council

Navy SEALS

GLOSSARY

agency: a government office that is in charge of all areas of government related to a particular topic. U.S. government agencies include the Department of Defense, the Department of State, the Department of Health and Human Services, and others.

bioterrorism: a form of terrorism that uses tiny living things called organisms to spread diseases

civilian: a citizen who is not serving in the military or in a police or fire-fighting department

counterintelligence agency: the part of government that works to stop enemy spies or to trick the enemy. For example, the CIA does counterintelligence work.

draft: a national system for selecting people to join the armed forces. The United States has not had a draft since 1973.

embassy: the official office of a government in another country. The United States has embassies in dozens of other countries.

epidemic: the outbreak of a disease that spreads quickly through a community, causing many people to get sick in a short period of time

national border: the official edge of a country

organized crime: complicated crimes committed by large groups of criminals. Organized crime includes earning money illegally and hiding it from the government.

prevent: to stop something from happening

recruit: a new member of the armed services

smuggle: to bring illegal items across a border

terrorism: acts of violence done by groups who are trying to force a government or other group of people to do what they want

vaccine: a tiny amount of a certain disease that is injected into a person's blood to help the person resist the full disease later

SELECTED BIBLIOGRAPHY

"About CDC." *Centers for Disease Control and Prevention.* N.d. <http://www.cdc.gov/aboutcdc.htm> (February 11, 2003).

Air Force Link. N.d. <http://www.af.mil> (February 11, 2003).

Border Patrol Overview. N.d. <http://www.ins.usdoj.gov/graphics/lawenfor/bpatrol/overview.htm> (February 11, 2003).

Federal Emergency Management Agency. N.d. <http://www.fema.gov> (February 11, 2003).

O'Hanlon, Michael E., et al. *Protecting the American Homeland: A Preliminary Analysis.* Washington, D.C.: Brookings Institute, 2002.

U.S. Department of Homeland Security. N.d. <http://www.dhs.gov/dhspublic/> (February 24, 2003).

U.S. Department of State. N.d. <http://www.state.gov> (February 11, 2003).

Wilson, James Q. *American Government: The Essentials.* New York: Houghton Mifflin College, 2000.

FURTHER READING AND WEBSITES

Air Force Kids Online
Website: <http://www.af.mil/aflinkjr/entrance.htm>
This fun, interactive site offers games, stories, and facts about the U.S. Air Force.

Bowen, Mary, and Monty Ruth. *To Be Safe During an Earthquake and Other Emergencies.* New York: To Be Safe, LLC, 2000.

BAM! Body and Mind
Website: <http://www.bam.gov>
This kids' site from the CDC provides young visitors with information on physical fitness, medical careers, and other health-related topics.

CIA's Homepage for Kids
Website: <http://www.odci.gov/cia/ciakids>
A history and overview of the CIA, along with puzzles and photographs, introduce visitors to this fascinating agency.

U.S. Bureau of Customs and Border Protection
http://cbp.gov
This website lists travel alerts, border crossing wait times, and other information about U.S. borders.

Dartford, Mark. *Fighter Planes*. Minneapolis, MN: Lerner Publications, 2004.

Doyle, Kevin. *Submarines*. Minneapolis, MN: Lerner Publications, 2004.

FBI Kids Page
Website: <http://www.fbi.gov/kids/k5th/kidsk5th.htm>
Your guides—trained FBI dogs Darrell and Shirley—take you on a tour of the Federal Bureau of Investigation.

FEMA for Kids
Website: <http://www.fema.gov/kids>
Check out this site for quizzes, trivia, and games taking a look at all the ways that FEMA helps us stay safe and healthy.

Harmon, Daniel E. *The U.S. Armed Forces*. New York: Chelsea House Publishers, 2001.

January, Brendan. *The FBI*. New York: Franklin Watts, 2002.

Learn About the State Department
Website: <http://www.state.gov/kids/learn>
This site gives basic information about the State Department and its role in keeping Americans safe.

Mark-Goldstein, Bonnie S., and Aviva Layton. *I'll Know What To Do: A Kid's Guide to Natural Disasters*. New York: Magination, 1997.

Official Website for the United States Marine Corps
Website: <http://www.usmc.mil>
Check out this site for a ton of information on the U.S. Marines.

The United States Army Homepage
Website: <http://www.army.mil>
You can find out all about the army at this official website.

U.S. Coast Guard
Website: <http://www.uscg.mil>
Learn about the Coast Guard's many responsibilities, from water safety to homeland security.

U.S. Navy's Official Web Site: Welcome Aboard
Website: <http://www.navy.mil>
This website introduces visitors to all areas of the Navy.

Yount, Lisa. *Epidemics*. New York: Lucent Books, 2000.

INDEX

Afghanistan, 25, 47
Alaska Patriot, 16
Aliganga, Sergeant Jesse, 45, 47
al-Qaeda, 25
anthrax, 43
Atlanta, Georgia, 39

bin Laden, Osama, 25
bioterrorism, 41, 43
Border Patrol, 13, 14, 15, 50
borders, 11–15
Briehl, Staff Sergeant Daniel, 45, 46
Bureau of Alcohol, Tobacco, Firearms, and
    Explosives (ATF), 46, 50
Bush, President George W., 18, 24, 33, 43. *See
    also* president, the

Canada, 11, 12, 13, 15
Centers for Disease Control and Prevention
    (CDC), 37–41, 43, 50
Central Intelligence Agency (CIA), 23, 50
China, 39–40
Civil War (1861–1865), 9
Columbia space shuttle, 33
Cuba, 12
Customs Service, 22, 50

Department of Homeland Security, 24, 50
Department of the Treasury, 46, 50
diseases. *See* public health
DNA, 22
draft, the, 9
"drop and cover", 27

earthquakes, 5, 27, 28
embassies, 44–48, 49
epidemics, 37, 40
Explosives Detection Canine Program, 20, 46

Federal Bureau of Investigation (FBI), 20–22,
    23, 25, 50

Federal Emergency Management Agency
    (FEMA), 27–28, 29, 31,32, 33, 34, 50
fingerprints, 22
fire departments, 19, 31–32, 34
floods, 27, 30, 31

Gerberding, Julie L., 37

Homeland Security Act, 24
Hoover, J. Edgar, 21
hurricanes, 29, 31, 32
Hussein, Saddam, 7

immigrants, 13, 14
Iraq, 2003 war in, 7, 47

Mexico, 11, 12, 13, 14
Miami, Florida, 29
Mississippi River, 31
mosquitoes, 36, 38, 39

Nairobi, Kenya, U.S. embassy in, 45, 46, 47.
    See also bin Laden, Osama
National Guard, 29–30, 31, 33, 34, 50
National Security Council, 20, 23, 50
natural disasters, 5, 10, 26–34, 49
Navy SEALS (SEa, Air, and Land), 10, 50
Niagara Falls, 11
Northridge Earthquake, 28

Office of Homeland Security, 24
organized crime, 21

Pembroke Pines, Florida, 34
Pentagon, the, 17–18
police departments, 19, 31–32, 34
polio, 42
pollution, 39
president, the, 23, 32
Project BioShield, 43
public health, 35–43, 49

Red Cross, 34
Ridge, Tom, 24

Saddam Hussein. *See* Hussien, Saddam
Salk, Jonas, 42
Salt Lake City, USS (ship), 8
San Andreas Fault, 28
SEALS (SEa, Air, and Land), Navy, 10
September 11, 5, 17–19, 21, 24, 25, 43
Severe Acute Respiratory Syndrome (SARS),
    39–40
smugglers, 12–13, 14, 15
special operations forces, 10
State Department. *See* U.S. Department of
    State
submarines, 8

Tanzania, U.S. embassy in, 47. *See also* bin
    Laden, Osama
terrorism, 5, 12, 17–22, 24, 25, 41, 46–47, 49
tornadoes, 26, 27

U.S. Air Force, 7, 9, 50
U.S. armed forces, 6–10, 12, 25, 50. *See also*
    U.S. Air Force; U.S. Army; U.S. Marine
    Corps; U.S. Navy
U.S. Army, 7, 8, 9, 10, 50
U.S. Coast Guard, 7, 15–16, 50
U.S Department of Defense, 8, 50
U.S. Department of Health and Human
    Services, 37, 50
U.S. Department of State, 23, 25, 48, 50
U.S. Environmental Protection Agency (EPA),
    39, 50
U.S. Marine Corps, 7, 9, 45, 46–48, 50
U.S. Navy, 7, 8, 9, 10, 50

vaccinations, 42, 49
Vietnam War, 9

wartime, 5, 6–9, 10, 49
West Nile Virus, 36–37, 38, 39, 43
World Trade Center, 17–18, 19
World Wars (1914–1918 and 1939–1945), 9

ABOUT THE AUTHOR

Sandy Donovan has written many books for young readers, on topics including history, civics, and biology. Donovan has also worked as a newspaper reporter and a magazine editor, and she holds a bachelor's degree in journalism and a master's degree in public policy. She has lived and traveled in Europe, Asia, and the Middle East. She lives in Minneapolis, Minnesota, with her husband and son. Donovan's other titles for Lerner include *Making Laws: A Look at How a Bill Becomes a Law* and *The Channel Tunnel.*

ACKNOWLEDGMENTS FOR QUOTED MATERIAL

p. 12, as quoted in "Text of Bush's Address," *CNN.com* (September 11, 2001, <http://www.cnn.com/2001/US/09/11/bush.speech.text>).

PHOTO ACKNOWLEDGMENTS

The photographs in this book are reproduced with the permission of: © Najlah Feanny/CORBIS SABA, pp. 4, 29; © Kevin Fleming/CORBIS, p. 6; U.S. Air Force, p. 7; U.S. Navy, p. 8; © Bettman/CORBIS, pp. 11, 21; © David Turnley/CORBIS, p. 13; © A&E/CORBIS SYGMA, p. 14; U.S. Coast Guard, p. 16; © Reuters NewMedia Inc./CORBIS, pp. 17, 24, 31, 33, 40, 47 (bottom); © Mark M. Lawrence/CORBIS, p. 19; © AFP/CORBIS, p. 20; © CORBIS Royalty Free, pp. 22, 32 (top), 35, 37; © H. Prinz/CORBIS, p. 23; National Oceanic and Atmospheric Administration (NOAA), p. 26; © Seattle Post-Intelligencer Collection, Museum of History & Industry/CORBIS, p. 27; © Roger Ressmeyer/CORBIS, p. 28; Federal Emergency Management Agency (FEMA), pp. 30, 32 (bottom), 34; Centers for Disease Control (CDC), pp. 39, 42; © Jeff Zaruba/CORBIS, p. 41; © Angelo Hornack/CORBIS, p. 44; © CORBIS SYGMA, p. 45; U.S. Marines, p. 47 (top).